Confessions
to a
Casino Joker

ENTERTAINERS

BERT BERTINO

Contents

Fine Dining And A Tenor

My New York mentor always had special gifts for his customers and his soulmates. He continually felt that the world's daily meetings should be an event and everything you do should intrigue and entice people to enjoy your company. This gentleman was a fine dressed silver fox who had spent over forty years in the gambling atmosphere of New York City, mostly as a "bookie." He was always well dressed, knew the elite of society and politicians of the world. He used his unique talents to spend time with the elite of casino gamblers, not necessarily because he wanted to but more because they wanted to enjoy his acquaintance. To have made his acquaintance is to have basked in the glow of true casino gaming royalty, as those who have shaking hands with him have made you elite in the annuls of gaming history.

On one sunny February afternoon, the silver fox and I were in New York City and took 12 customers of his, to a famous restaurant right near Carnegie Hall. As we sat and conversed, we were in the back of the room, not the most advantageous place to be. This was highly unusual for this gentleman to arrange something that was not Grade A, top-flight. Rather he had placed us in a rear table, far from the center of the room (his domain), that sat 12 people in the back of the restaurant space, which never happened before to my knowledge with him. After about twenty minutes of conversation, where everybody was intrigued and able to order their cocktails and their lunches, we were now beginning to be entertained by a bolstering tenor voice coming from the back wall where we were seated.

We soon realized that the Premier tenor of the entire universe was serenading us while he was rehearsing for his evening performance. Yes, we were on the back wall of Carnegie Hall and listening to an hour of practice for an opera superstar that everyone was clamoring to get tickets for. This was the silver fox's highlight for his customers as he could only obtain four tickets for the event but was able to give twelve premier players an opportunity that they would never have been able to enjoy. Through expansive networks that he had set up in over forty years is how he was aware of the opportunity and booked the table to "Always be in the right place at the most opportune time".

And even though this gentleman is long gone and many other people there in the room have passed on this was a great day and resonates in my mind nearly for your thirty-five years later. The silver fox had an extreme gravelly voice that always said, "know your environment, know your people and always anticipate what they want." On this day he far exceeded all the knowledge needed.

Suits and Tuxedos

While my New York mentor, the Silver Fox mentioned earlier, was well known within the gaming community throughout the United States and he always drew back on his east coast roots to entice patrons and entertainment megastars. Much of the time we spent together, he was always in his uniform of blue suit, white crisp shirt and red tie. Even when we traveled to Las Vegas to work with west coast operations, he kept to his attire. Many of our employer's fellow operation's executives dressed in polo shirts and casual slacks. We however were distinguished by our suits and ties much of the time that I was in his company, and I followed suit and still continually wear a shirt and tie even though we were in meetings with very casual fellow employees.

For the ten years we worked together, I always found his professionalism and knowledge to be of great strength to me and others. He never ceased to expound upon knowledge and teaching opportunities to better serve the casino organization he was affiliated with and to help young future executives like myself. Many times, he was short with many of the other executives within the organization because his knowledge far exceeded theirs and became upset when they said things he did not agree with. However, with me and a few of my fellow junior executives we were always able to have his ear and at the same time suggest things that we thought would be proper. Many times, he would help us through our thought process and at the same time he was never short but always willing to help. I have always attempted to keep his legacy when helping others and speaking with executives who have little knowledge but the correct family connections.

Many years after we had worked together, we met up in Las Vegas at a Grand Opening event for a new casino and again the tenor that we spoke of earlier was performing. And instead of the uniform of blue suit, white shirt and red tie, he was bedazzled in his white hair with a black tuxedo and a red tie. He was at the pinnacle of his career and was happy to have myself and others who he had mentored with him at this occasion. He gently nudged me and another former mentee to join him briefly backstage. As we approached the area he had designated, he introduced both of us to the musicians, the stage manager and finally the performer. He explained to everyone there why he had chosen the performance personally and why this was to be his swan song in entertainment.

This was one of the last times I saw the silver fox in good health and about two years prior to our last meeting in Florida prior to his death. He was a strong force in my life and someone I have emulated throughout my career and continue to hear his gravelly voice instructing me on the right way.

The Superstar Swap

There once was my Catskills mentor, who was much more than a counselor, guide, tutor and teacher. He was my guru for all things marketing, entertainment, promotions, and special events. He did not know how to do a small event; he only knew what over-the-top looked like and how to interact with everyone so his vision could be realized. This guru had the wonderful knack of always trying to resolve whatever problem was set before him. I genuinely enjoyed working with this shaman because he was the man who always came up with the answers no matter what the question may be.

I have tried to model my life after him and have succeeded on some fronts. His belief in himself was infectious and his belief in the team he assembled was contagious. When he needed to make changes and pivot the organizations goals and structure, the faith that his fellow upper management and his subordinates made for flawless transitions. While he worked with many to improve the organization, his laser focus on growing me and my potential will never be forgotten. (During the period I worked directly for him, I was attending my final years of college to attain a marketing bachelor's degree. He insisted on reviewing all material I was presenting to my professors, and grading my presentations prior to me turning them in. These are the days prior to word processors and computers, so a minor change needed to force the entire page to be retyped. He not only forced me to be a better student, but a better employee and person.)

One of my favorite mornings spent with the guru from the Catskills was sitting in his office as a junior executive with six other of my compatriots and a phone call came in saying that the well-known country entertainer that was coming to perform that weekend had fell and broke his leg. Without a modicum of doubt and /or a bead of sweat he hung up the phone picked it up again and called another member of the troop that always performed at our casino and proceeded to convince this major crooner to come in three days from then and perform for the weekend in return for using dates later in the year. To the amazement of everyone in the room, this was done with ease, poise, and respect to everyone. This made making telephone calls to customers of high wealth much easier as they had already made their reservations to come for the weekend and needed to be aware of the sudden change.

The telephone calls went well for the remainder of the day, as an entire force of player development executives were pressed into service to make the announcement of the changes. This is long before social media and email, so the grunt work of reaching two thousand people in one day, prior to the announcement of the accident on the evening news, was imperative. Most customers were intrigued by the change, some were shocked by the late notice, and all wanted additional seats. Everyone was accommodated in the best fashion imaginable, and the weekend was a larger success than anticipated. This was accomplished because of one man who believed not only in his ability but also the capability of the entire team that worked for him.

Big Voice In A Black Hat

In Country music there are many Great voices and entertainers who fill the vast void of gravel voiced performer, but the man in the black hat as a singer was extraordinary and as a story teller would bring people to their feet in applause and knees in laughter. This man towered over many and brings enjoyment to all. He was boisterous, irreverent and fun loving on stage while he performed a solid set of old and new hits while giving his fans even more than they had bargained for. When off stage he was a pleasant consoling gentleman who was willing to spend time and effort to be with his fans taking pictures and telling stories about his life. On the golf course he was a fierce competitor who rarely would miss the opportunity to enjoy the game of kings. I remember one time he was booked at a resort in the Midwest and barely parked his bus as he jumped off the motorcoach, grabbed his golf clubs and went out for a round of 18 holes prior to even checking into the hotel or having a bite to eat. He traveled many times to visit casinos that I worked at and performed, and there always wondering what the golf situation was and how to enjoy at least two rounds during his performances.

While on the golf course, he would often interact with other golfers and wave, tell stories and take pictures. On one particular round, The Black Hat was prominent and he was having a great time. He is a giant of a man and known to wallop a golf ball quite a way down the fairway. As normal during his performance weekends, guests, fans and fellow golfers would flock to see and talk with him. While we tried to keep this to a minimum, he was easy to see and hard to hide. One particular spring day this was the truth and was backing up the golfers behind him. Many did not mind, but a particular golfer, who's wife was a high roller, was offended by the time being taken. Black Hat waved the group behind him to play ahead, including the loud husband of the high roller. Few words were exchanged but a nasty smerk and a rude comment was made by the golfer. Black Hat took it in stride and continued to enjoy his round while entertaining the fellow golfers.

About two holes after the foursome passed, Black Hat took a drive at a massive par five, and was waved on by the loud golfer. Of course, the golfer was not paying attention, and got "beaned" in the head with a mighty drive. Soon the screaming started and the Black Hat rushed to his side to apologize. As I was there in Black Hat's foursome, I had observed the entire encounter all day. The loud golfer was screaming first at Black Hat and then at me. When mentioned that he had waved us on, he admitted he did not think anyone could hit that far. He then decided to calm down and realized that this person must be of importance because I was with him and playing golf (something I am not good at and rarely do). When the round ended, loud golfer proceeded to leave without knowing who hit him.

Later that evening, while being seated for the concert, he complained to his wife and friends about this big guy with a Black Hat, hitting him with a golf ball. When he saw me, he brought up the "beaning" but his wife told him to be quiet. I laughed and quickly moved him from the third row to front row center. His wife deserved the upgrade and the Black Hat would truly enjoy his show much more. As the performance began, Black Hat immediately noticed the loud golfer and dedicated a love song to his wife, while drinking songs were dedicated to loud golfer. The proceeding meet and greet was hysterical and even had Black Hat pointing down on the bump he had left.

Country Singing Goddess

There once was a country performer that lived in New York City and had a weekend performance with a casino in Atlantic City. I had to be in Manhattan, on this fine spring day and was about to take a limousine back to Atlantic City when I was notified that this performer was also going back and would I mind sharing a limousine with her. I was proud to join in and sat in the front seat while her and her friends sat in the back and serenaded myself and the driver for the ride to Atlantic City.

As the goddess was well known to me and the driver, listening to versions of her most popular songs done AL Capela, was a great indulgence and something I would never forget. The chance to attend her concerts were always a treat but being entertained in a small compartment traveling down the highway was beyond anything that either of us could have ever imagined. We listened to stories attached to the songs she was singing. She reminisced on other performers who she had sung with and who helped her. She also reminisced on those she had helped along with their careers, and how when she reached stardom (my words not hers), goddess felt obligated to help others with their career. She waxed poetically about helping people to get their songs published, sung and albums to be made. She sang their songs and then invited them to sing along to get better known. To this day, she is the goddess to many performers who worked their way through Music City and reached their dreams as a result of what the goddess had done for them.

Then she reached on the floor of the limo and took out her guitar. She went to town, and her friends joined in. I of course kept my mouth shut as the wheel barrel I need to carry a tune was unavailable. The guitar resonated throughout the cabin as she did not tone down her volume for the environment. She however belted out tune after tune and tried new versions of old songs. We were her private audience and she wished we would critique. Of course that was not going to happen as that is not what I am proficient at, rather I know what I like and she was the performer I truly loved.

This goddess was a true pleasure to be around, she smiled, she laughed and joked with us and then somewhere around the middle of the trip she questioned if there was a place where she may be able to go to the lavatory. Well because of her celebrity status we just couldn't pull into any rest stop, so we found a police barracks on the Garden State Parkway and pulled in with this big white limousine. I approached barracks, gently opened the door and walked inside to a full room of state troopers and ask if we could use the restroom and I told him who was in the car. They all laughed, they all joked and I said if you don't believe me come out to the car which some of them did. They of course did not believe me but a lucky trooper who came to the car and escorted the goddess to her refuge. When they realized I was not kidding they escorted her in and she serenaded them with a couple songs and had a very good time. There must have been a dispatcher somewhere as the troopers in the barracks multiplied during her visit.

It was a half hour delay, but it made the trip so much fun and the lives of fifteen to twenty State troopers truly delighted to indulge in music of an Icon and the persona of the goddess.

Loser Rock Band

Entertainers are always an interesting breed to deal with. Sometimes when you were dealing with former rock legends from years ago, who never gave up their bad habits, and believe they are bigger than their fans and the organizations that employ them. Many of the hair bands of the 1980's and 1990's never encountered organizations who told them NO and never meet promoters who would penalize them for bad behavior. Some bands have realized that times have changed, music has changed and organizations that partake in their brand and times of music are few and far between. They are also connected by many of the people who work in these organizations. Good shows and positive customer reactions are shared. Bad shows are also shared and limit future bookings.

Casinos utilize the "hair bands" to attract an up-and-coming demographic of new patrons who are younger and are taking hard earned money and valuable time to find new forms of entertainment. This demographic is fragile and needs to be developed properly and reaching out with music of their era is important to developing a bond. This new demographic had reached a level of dispensary income to enjoy newer forms of entertainment that previously may not have been available.

One band that was highly sought after and an organization that I worked with, genuinely wanted them to perform. The band members came in from across the country and as we were in the Midwest, logistics was important. One of the band mates who had not given up his bad habits of many years was coming from Los Angeles; he was flying into Denver before reaching his destination near the casino. When the performer was to reach the destination, he never showed up. It was later found out that he never left Los Angeles, but he hid in the bathroom of LAX not to make the performance. His bandmates were in soundcheck when they realized he was nowhere to be found. The concert had to be canceled. Everybody had to be refunded their money and the gaming customers had to be compensated for their inconvenience. The only reaction that the Band had was that this was sad but typical of him and the only route reaction of the bad party band member was "I just didn't feel like coming."

The projected audience was disappointed and angry at the band and the organization. They felt baited by the casino resort when announcements were made five hours prior to the performance. Social media was a life savior to get the word out as well as explain the situation. When customers finally understood the situation and how the one band member caused this entire fiasco, their anger turned to the lead singer and not the band nor the resort, rightfully so.

This sad situation that fractured the band, that never performed again, but chasing the money advanced was interesting. The expenditure for lights, sound and promotions could never be recouped. The band's good-will that they had with their fans was never resolved and my large mouth along with several promoter friends resolved to reach the ends of the earth to never allow the band to be hired again. The network of promotors and booking organizations along with organizations that housed concerts quickly cancelled the future shows. There was a proposal offered to the band, that if they replaced the lead singer, there would be further opportunities, but they never resolved to replace their problem child.

Night Of The Stars

In the mid-1980s, a prominent lead singer from a disco / R&B group, separated from his bandmates and wanted to start a solo career. He had a few hits independently by penning songs for other performers and was now branching out into a solo career to further his dynasty. This lead singer had a knack of writing love songs that were commercially successful and received a great deal of radio-airtime. This made the transition to a solo career quite an easy evolution, along with having songs sang by other famous artists, giving him the credit, he deserved.

Just prior to his launch of a solo career, I was in Las Vegas and had the opportunity to join him and another famous musical artist (in previous story referred to as Mom's favorite singer). They were collaborating on a song that would be a huge success for both. They had a window of twenty-four hours prior to being recorded as a duet. They both were excited and hurried simultaneously, but happy to be together, and I was elated to just be in the room. They both released in the next month an album (yea it was that long ago) that contained this song. Each album received critical success, but the song they collaborated on was a hit and skyrocketed on the pop, R&B, country and Hot 100 charts of Billboard Magazine.

During the same period of time, there was a woman who had separated from her family band and was restarting her career to the excitement of many. She was a hard driving rock singer who was also pursuing the solo route and needed to be revealed as the true mega star that she was. This true lady needed the break to give the public the realization that her brand was strong, and her career was about to have a soaring meteoric rise. Her first solo album revealed her magic and became a commercial success quickly.

Together they were offering a weekend of pure entertainment. When they were booked, the package was a risk by an entertainment genius who knew each would be successful, together they would be dynamite. The Friday evening show went very well, and everyone enjoyed the two solo performers who did a few duets at the crossover between her opening and his continuance of the show. On Saturday the crossover was very exciting and then the female opening act proceeded to go to her dressing room during the male performers part of the show. He had done duets with quite a few performers and the Queen Diva joined him on stage for an extremely popular song that they made prominent for a movie. They proceeded to do two or three other songs of hers, to the delight of the audience. Later in the show, Mom's Favorite Singer, came on stage and sang their version of the duet together.

For the finale all the performers came out on stage and did three songs to the delight of the entire Audience and to excitement of management. Because the venue had limited seating, I watched the entire show from the stage wings and realized I was enjoying an enchanted evening across every musical category. The limited number of guests who enjoyed this night would talk about this far into the future as the evening they saw all these mega-stars together. The owner of the resort had become a prominent figure in the casino and the entertainment arenas and bolstered his reputation that evening. Within a year of this magical night, each of the performers were selling out stadiums and other venues. This was truly a NIGHT OF THE STARS.

The Blues Man

Over the course of my career working in the casino industry, I always had the joy of working with blues singers and artists, especially when working in the Southern and Midwest United States. One of the performers that I absolutely loved working with was a hard playing, hard drinking, fun loving blues guitar player who was beloved by his fans and everyone who ever had a chance to meet him. His colorful dress always distinguished him on stage and walking across the facility he loved performing to both small and large crowds. The Blues Man would very often enter the audience and play remotely throughout entire venue. He always felt that the people in the back of the audience deserved the same show and respect that the people upfront we're getting so therefore he would walk around through the entire arena and play and entertain different sections.

During one specific show, he walked throughout the audience for about 15 minutes and ended up in the back of the room at the bar playing for the bartenders and then ordered a drink and quickly said "whoops sorry I am supposed to be on stage now" and proceeded to file through the audience again and ended up on stage. His musical prowess and his quick hands entertained many different variants of audiences throughout the world. Although I had not made his acquaintance until he was later in life, I had been a lifelong fan and knew his musicality would entertain many differing audiences and attract new fans wherever he was booked.

Another show that he performed, was in a Deep South, at a riverboat casino. This was his home turf, and he performed like the show would never end. Being in the entertainment business for many years, he had countless friends who would visit and take in a show from time to time. On this evening, a few of his compatriots joined him on stage for an impromptu jam session. This brought the audience to their feet, stomping and cheering and would have sunk the riverboat if the venue were not safely land based.

After the show, we expected a short meet-and-greet with The Blues Man, but instead he had other plans in mind. He proceeded to invite everyone in the showroom to visit him and his friends at the casino lounge to take photos and to "chat." He did his photo opportunity with the high rollers in private and then proceeded to go to the casino lounge. Fifteen hundred potential guests in a lounge that could hold two hundred was about to turn into a security nightmare. Instead, he stood in the back of the casino lounge and smiled for photographs, signed swag that was sold during the show and just took moments to make people feel that they were important to him, which they were. From a resort organization standpoint, we wanted to give a great experience to our guests, and The Blues Man delivered.

The British Invader

During the 1960s the British invasion brought us many great performers and bands that had taken Europe by storm. This was the evolution of a variant in Rock and Roll that everyone became entranced by. Decades later, the trance is still very active and brings many customers to establishments that offer the music of that era especially with entertainers that are still willing to perform together in full force.

One of my favorites was a lesser recognized band but had many hits during the invasion period. One day in Las Vegas, my friends and I were visiting a rival casino for a excursion party. While sitting at a slot machine, playing video poker, they made announcements that this performer and his band would be appearing all week long in the show room.I proceeded to sing one of their more popular tunes while playing my slot machine (as I mentioned previously, I rarely bring along the wheel barrel needed for me to carry a tune).I imagined that I sang loud enough that I could enjoy but really not interrupting many people around me.Unfortunately, halfway through the chorus I turned and saw this slight gentleman sitting one seat over for me laughing and I realized this was the British invader that made this song famous.We laughed, we joked (mostly about my voice) and we exchanged phone numbers saying that I always look for entertainment and would love to have him and his band entertain my casino guests across the country. Over the course of the next few years, the performer and his band appeared a few times and we always reminisced fondly about the afternoon in Las Vegas and the laughs that we shared.

During one particular show in the upper Midwest, the British Invader's band was unavoidably detained by a severe snowstorm and would be about a half hour late for the show.Not to disappoint our audience, he proceeded to serenade the audience with songs by other entertainers from the same era. You would expect that his British accent would not carry over into songs that much of the audience knew from the original artists, but be it pop, country and R&B, it pulled it off perfectly. As he was performing, much of it Alca pela, as he only had his own guitar, many audience members funneled in and were completely taken aback by the performer's range. Once his bandmates arrived, the show brought down the house and truly solidified my use of their services again and again.

After the show, the British Invader was excited for what had just occurred and said he always wanted to sing other performers songs on stage, and occasionally would include one but not and entire set. As I have seen since, fifty years after coming to America, he was justly happy in his own skin. Many perform-ers would have postponed their show or even cancelled for the evening. This was not an option for him, as this may have been the first time that a patron may have witnessed him, and his band live after many decades of buying their records. This is a true showman and someone who has become a good friend.

The Crooner

The crooner like many of his counter parts of the Big Band era, always had a low tone voice and told a particularly good sentimental story. On the other side he was a hard living, hard partying, enjoyable man that I had the privilege to work with many times over a twenty-year period. I eventually even worked with some of his offspring also. The Crooner lived in an era when the media was always kind to performers, but not always him. His life was always broadcast across print and television networks. Had he lived in the era with social media, his success would have never survived. While others lived lives of a relative bubble, the Crooner's exploits were always front and center to his fans. This in some respects kept him in their focus and only extended his brand

and the interest he generated. He became an icon for this and many other reasons.

He sometimes would come alone but normally brought friends along that would entertain and enriched the environment that he was trying to create.He was well known to have worked with many of the musical greats as he was the recognized as the supreme of pure audio performers.I had the privilege to work with him at eight casino resort properties across many states during my differing tenures with varied organizations. He believed that the harder you worked the harder you should play, and it was a great analogy for life and for entertainment.

During one fun filled week in which he had four shows, filmed two television commercials, and hosted a seventieth birthday party for a fellow performer (with a guestlist that was the who's-who of entertainment royalty), I witnessed a mountain of an entertainer.During his stage performances, he showcased his genuine personality, singing many of his chart-topping hits but also covering other performers songs to pay tribute to their craft.He personified the gambler's ideal of an all-around entertainer who was not only seen on stage but in the bar and gambling on the casino floor.As he was known to partake in casino action, he was the perfect catalyst to seduce gamblers and vacationers to a casino resort (and he did in legions of fans).During a long filming session, the Crooner became annoyed by the length of times it was taking to complete a simple scene.As I was an assistant to him for this commercial filming, I was taking the brunt of his frustrations.Luckily for me, the organization I worked for, valued my input and my ear to what the customer and the client wanted.I took his concerns, quickly excused myself, gave my input and returned in a timely matter as not to enrage the Crooner further.The commercial was a success, the result of the advertisement campaign yielded results far surpassing expectations and was nominated for an advertising Clio award.The awards dinner was fabulous, winning in our category was a dream realized, being the fifth person on a team that was presented four statues has only made me strive harder for a return engagement (nine AAF Gold Awards, but not a Clio yet).

I was always the kid in the environment and just soaked in all the bliss that was brought, however as we both aged, I became a trusted crutch at times when people felt the crooner was failing, he will always be remembered to me as the greatest of all times. There will always be a debate of who was a better singer, who was a better actor and who was a better person but there will never be any thought as to who was a better friend, person, or confidant. He enjoyed the casino environment as many people would like to sit and relax in a rocking chair he was always at home behind the microphone, in front or behind of the casino gaming table and sitting there smoking a cigarette and enjoying whiskey.

After his passing many people reflected on what he had done for the entertainment industry I only reflect on what he had done for casino entertainment and especially for me as I learned at his knee about what the magnitude of mega-stardom resembled.

The Duchess Diva

There once was a female breakout pop and R&B group that had many hits.After a few albums, the Queen Diva began a solo career and left the group rudderless.The Duchess Diva, having taken over for the Queen Diva after her departure, continued the trio of singers.She was always believed to be the second banana, unfortunately for her, she never received the accolades and the recognition nor the prominence that her sister in singing had received. As the years went on, she continued her career singing the songs they had made the group popular but many of which she cannot claim as her own.She had never developed a substantial solo career for herself and was relegated to the remix charts and opening for more prominent performers.

On an enjoyable evening in the Midwest, she was performing with members of the R&B Kings mentioned previously and proceeded to overrun her allotted time because she felt that her voice and her entertainment was more important than theirs. This was unfortunate because there is only so much a lot of time for the show before the customers wanted to go back to the casino floor. She was beautiful in appearance and voice but however she was malicious in her intent. During her set, it was determined that she would be running over so I made the decision to bring up the lights in the arena and cut off her mike. From the rear of the arena our Master of Ceremonies thank her and said the the R&B Kings will be coming to the stage after a brief intermission. This did not please the Duchess Diva and she immediately was prepared to make a scene. As the R&B Kings are true gentleman, they did not want any part of this and as I made the decision, I took the brunt of her yelling in the dressing room. She wanted more time and her manager was belligerent about what we had done. Explaining how much time was allotted to her and her lack of consideration for the audience and for her fellow performers finally came down to providing her a copy of her signed contract and the amount of time she was to perform.

The R&B Kings were gracious and allowing her time but had to cut down their show to accommodate her overage in musical talent. The story spread fast and wide and soon she was relegated to either performing solo or not allowed to be an opening act any further at least for larger acts that demanded more time and attention. This was a sorry situation and she had learned poor habits from her management and her previous record labels who tried to appease her because of her thrust into the spotlight, due to the Queen Diva's departure. I did not wish to disrespect this talented performer but at the same time much of the audience paid for the R&B Kings.

The Empress Of Country Music

The Empress was an absolute delight to work with over the many years that she performed at casino resorts that I worked within. Her modest upbringing with many siblings caused an overwhelming fear of poverty and returning to her roots.She was always concerned with how the homeless throughout the areas she entertained were treated and how her notoriety could help the local situation.She was a tireless advocate of improvements needed for the homeless and had performed to raise money for this cause.She would donate proceeds from her "swag table" (CD's, t-shirts, posters, etc....) to benefit local charities that supported the downtrodden and homeless.

There are diverse articles written about her and her family and the vast environments of the resorts they performed in. However, nothing is more exciting than watching her strut on stage and sing her mega hits one after another, until she finally culminated in her greatest tune of all.Many of her accompanists were her sons, daughters, sisters, and grand-children who always performed to the great-est of their ability, but everybody came to see the Empress. Many of the people that enjoyed her music came for the sheer magic of sharing the room with her. Countless multitudes of her fans had been following her most of their lives and believe that they were truly witness-ing greatness.

The Empress was a diminutive woman who through the years had become frail and aged but still gave a performance like no other.When I saw her in the earlier part of her career, she would stand center stage and belt out music for well over two hours, but as she matured, she was confined to sitting and singing her tunes from a leather tufted chair in the center of the stage.

The Empress always entered stage left, escorted by a family member talking about how overwhelmed she was that people still came out to see her.I have never seen a performance by her that was not standing room only.She would now proceed to sit in her big chair and talk and sing of life.On one evening, she was in a particular feisty mood and sang with bravado and power that her fans enjoyed immensely.Once she reached her final and most famous of melodies, she stood and sang powerfully to the audience and proceeded to reach all sectors of the stage.As she completed the song, she waved goodbye and exited the stage, got on her motorcoach, and rushed away.We later found out that she was experiencing chest pains for the last fifteen minutes but did not want to disappoint her fandom and she had her appropriate medicine in the motorcoach on the way to the hospital.

Her quick departure was stunning, but her performance was still exciting and enriching to all fans that attend.Once the news was released that she had a medical emergency, everyone in attendance gained the ultimate respect for the Empress of Country Music.

The Fiddler

Throughout my career I have worked with many country artists who had great range in both voice and instrumental prowess.One performer comes to mind who is exceptional with every string instrument imaginable, best known for playing electric violin and prancing around the stage even in his advanced years. He was for many of his songs, a skilled guitar player with a deep husky voice, but one song always brought the house down and later years became his grand finale or at least his last encore that utilized his signature electric violin.He was strong with a banjo and guitar and a gravel voice that encouraged numerous fans to want to sing along. He rarely performed less than two hours and always brought the house down no matter the venue throughout the United States. He was a true gentleman to work with and always a joy on or off the stage.

During a tour that swung through the Southwest and West Coast I was able to enjoy the Fiddler and his band in three separate venues wile working with my organization. His show list varied between venues but was a crisp and raw at each stop on the tour. He believed that he could cater his play list to the specific venue and make everyone happy, even changing up songs mid-show. He also believed that every person he was entertaining, was his guest and gave the respect they deserved while on stage.

During a extremely hot evening in Arizona, he was warm and sweating profusely, but continued to delight the fandom that was that evening's audience. A patron who had imbibed in a little too much libation began to heckle the Fiddler. At this point midway through the show, the Fiddler played his songs without giving much attention to the heckler, which only enraged and the disgruntled fan more. Because the heckler was close to the stage, he was shielded from quick access by security.As security forces closed in, the Fiddler began to play directly above the heckler and the sound team pumped up the volume as to drown out anything but the music.Once security scooped up the heckler, the Fiddler went into a feverous performance of music and dance.Many had no idea what had occurred, and the Fiddler did not expound upon the occurrence.

The Greasey Rock-N-Roller (Mom's Favorite Singer)

When I was growing up there was the Steel Pier in Atlantic City New Jersey, that had entertainment seven days a week. It was an especially great place to go on a rainy day as they always had two movies (mostly first run), headline shows in the Grand Showroom and they built a large venue in the back overlooking the water, "The Golden Dome." The Dome had new and upcoming acts, and always caught patrons heading out to the water acrobats, the diving horse, and the Diving Bell. At the time I never realized that this venue fed my desire to produce entertainment and to be in the heart of performances.

One day when my family was at the pier enjoying ourselves, my mom took me at the ripe age of eight years old, to see the diving horse. The up-and-coming show we stumbled upon was a group performing rock 'n' roll music that my mother did not appreciate, and the lead singer was dressed in black leather with long straggly beard, greasy black hair and motorcycle leather vest and chaps.She truly did not want me to stay, so we watched two songs and then she snatched me of out the Dome, never to see this band again.Let us fast forward about twelve years and now I have joined the casino industry, and my mother's favorite performer was appearing at the organization I was employed with.I made the necessary purchase of tickets with my employee discount and arranged for mom and dad to have primo seats for her favorite act.

It just so happened to be that this white haired, clean cut, country singer who my mother absolutely loved listening to, was the same performer that she yanked me away from little over more than a decade prior.After the show, mom was so happy to have seen him in person and so up close and personal, that I requested that she be able to join a meet and greet with him.My relationships allowed for her to join in with me escorting her along to the private reception (sorry dad but you wanted to play craps anyway). During the encounter, mom's favorite was kind, soothing and extremely easy to speak with, and mom loved the situation we were in.At one point mom mentioned that this was the first time she had seen him in concert, and not wanting to correct her I chuckled.However, as we walked away, I explained that this man was the GREASEY ROCK- N-ROLLER from Steel Pier, who was the same person she just shook hands with and took a photo opportunity alongside.Mom was so happy to have seen her favorite but so angry she missed the previous opportunity to enjoy because of her pre-conceived notions.

Having seen this entertainer numerous times now, I still am transported back to the two occasions when an eight-year-old briefly enjoyed rock music and the way I made my mom feel when she saw her favorite singer.

The Illusionist's Finger

Casinos are always very well known to have magicians and illusionist perform in their showrooms. The mystery and mystique of illusion has been a casino staple pre-dating Harry Houdini. As the expansion of casino gaming throughout the world, entertainment through the enchantment of illusion has proliferated to all ends of the earth. In the early days of theatre and circus, magic was always a staple of the performances. Now it is a free standing staple of many entertainment calendars.

One of my favorites of all time has granted cars to appear and disappear on stage, large pachyderms appear from nowhere and letting him disappear from the stage and reappear in the back of the showroom. These are always fun and exciting illusions to enjoy, however, the greatest illusion is when a performer does something so extraordinary that the audience is left awestruck.

The illusionist I am thinking of had a brilliant act in which he had an audience member cut a section of rope and then it mysteriously was re-tied together without any knots, this is always exciting and continually permitted the audience to truly leave the show in amazement. Unfortunately, this time, the audience member who cut the rope, ended up cutting the illusionists' fingertip. As the magnificent illusionist reacted and said, "oh well, she just cut the tip of my finger off," everybody applauded and thought it was the greatest illusion imaginable, unfortunately the curtains closed, and he was rushed to the hospital to reattach the tip of his finger. Many of the audience sat in amazement that the show had ended so abruptly. The entire audience was given a raincheck for the next evening, as the showroom was to be dark, and this would have been considered a make-up. Not many of the audience members complained, and about ninety percent returned the next evening for the make-up show.

The illusionist immediately contacted the resort management to arrange the additional show as to not disappoint his supporters. Many of the patrons who attended the show had seen him previously, but some had only heard of his prowess and wanted to experience him firsthand. As a fan myself, I had seen his performances previously and did not see this unfortunate occurrence. I instead attended the next evening's magical presentation and was in awe of how he performed so acutely with a bandage on his hand.

Considering that only a third of the show had occurred, this was going to be a special evening. The continuation of the illusionist act was performed with additional slight of hands added to enrich the performance while trying new fantasies that were for future performances. Everything went very well until the finale. While the grand finale would still occur, the "Finale" was announced and the same patron from the previous evening was brought out to cut the rope. Humor abounded as she was presented a child's safety scissors and everyone erupted in laughter. The illusion was performed and everyone in the audience was treated to a bonus group of bewitching, to the delight of the resort management and to the entertainer himself.

The Ladies Of Burlesque

In different venues, burlesque has become a redefined and resurgent form of entertainment that was re-discovered and brought to the forefront by some incredibly famous performers and then spread across the country by companies of female performers with outstanding vocal and physical talents. Many critiques of burlesque consistently refer to the performances as "stripper shows" but they far exceed the sexual titillation that is most well-known. Rather, the sexual tension of the shows only further the entertainment experiences that are offered and the recreation that surrounds the exploits only greater enrich the casino's theatrical menu. Many customers do not frequent reviews or certain genres of musicians, rather this is another entertainment offering that attracts an additional patron demographic.

Many states have laws and statues against forms of sexual teasing and the various forms of undress that is allowable. In a nutshell, burlesque allowed for many performances to occur in these jurisdictions, that were titillating and enticing but not overtly offensive to the audience and the local legislatures. Many differing apparatuses have been utilized from feather boas all the way to giant sized cocktail glasses. The props utilized only added to the intrigue and the entertainment value and were highly sought after in many jurisdictions where "blue-laws" were in effect. The demographic of the audience also intrigued me as you would almost always have a higher concentration of couples and ladies attending. Many of the woman present were accompanying their significant others to enhance their present and hopefully future romantic experiences. Some men attended singularly but they were few and far between and were quick to make an exit after the performance.

One of the funniest experiences I have ever observed was a gentleman in his seventies, thoroughly entertained by the ladies on stage. He was intrigued by the entertainment value and with sharp attention, rarely diverted his eyes from the stage or his favorite artist. As the performers entered the audience, his favorite artist, grabbed a hold of his hand and began to dance with him while his wife being offended that he was performing, grabbed him by the other hand and pulled him out of the show room. He glanced back at his favorite artist, with the expression of a five-year-old child in the toy aisle, being drug out of the store by the hand. I am unsure if their future romantic experiences were enhanced, rather I believe his embarrassment was exacerbated.

The Guys Who Danced And The Girls Who Observed

Having worked in the casino industry throughout the country, I was always amazed by the male dancing entertainers that performed in small and large venues. I constantly saw the clubs that held them and how many women that flocked to enjoy in Las Vegas and Atlantic City. It continuously amazed me how the artists would perform night after night to half-filled showrooms in the major destination resorts in these gaming meccas. When I began to work with the tribal casinos in the South and Midwest, I was consistently shocked by the overabundance of patrons, especially women, flocking to the shows and dancing on the tables and trying to tear the clothes off the entertainers. I realize that every jurisdiction is different, but these smaller venues would have to schedule three and four shows over a weekend to accommodate the numerous amounts of patrons that desired entrance (some for multiple shows).

One evening I accidentally entered the show room prior to the finale, when the doors were flung open, and everybody came flocking out. I was truly afraid for my life by these patrons looking to molest the closest male character they encountered. As a short, fat guy in a suit, I was going to be fodder for these attendees, and I ran for my life (lol). This crowd of invigorated patrons made their way through the facility and proceeded to insight encounters with gentleman they knew (and some they did not). The second show of the evening was not far different, as the show-room patrons were in search of companion-ship after an invigorating period of lap-danc-ing and table romping. What fascinated me the most about this evening was that I had seen the showroom patrons from other destination casinos react so far differently than what occurred this evening, and immediately renewed a contract for a future set of performances six month in advance.

While the patrons who attended the burlesque shows in a previous story had exited calmly and proceeded to continue their evening with cocktails, dinners and gaming entertainment, these patrons invigorated by the dancing gentleman, attacked the facility in the way a boxing match or MMA event energizes the venue. Vitality is an important part of what energizes a casino resort, and this form of entertainment in certain jurisdictions, genuinely excites the casino floor. The electric in the air can turn a quiet night of gambling into a momentous night of enjoyment. Casino resorts are built for release and for a location to be entertained. Casino resorts are relatively new to the entertainment genre but places for release and total decadence have been around since the days of the romans where entertainment, spas and games of chance were the release for the rich and powerful. Casinos have given this to the multitudes and this is another form of release that we all need.

The Princess Diva

During The Queen Diva's career sabbatical, for poor relations with most of the agents and venues she had performed within, she moved to Europe and left the entertainment industry for nearly ten years. The Queen Diva became a precautionary tale for other performers who thought treating fans and venues poorly would be tolerated. The Queen Diva had performed throughout the world and was highly respected but could not get a booking nor a soundtrack label to record her and release an album (tape and CD).

At this time, The Princess Diva's entertainment prowess came to prominence, and she shot up the music charts as well as dominating stage, screen, and television. The Princess Diva while having strong roots within the musical sorority was more concerned with the minor trappings of success then giving her fans enjoyable performances. I remember one famous August night, when the Princess Diva decided that air-conditioning would hurt her voice, so therefore instructed the casino resort to have no air-conditioning within the entertainment venue. It was summer with humidity and temperature exceeding 90° and many customers stayed to enjoy one or two songs before total heat exhaustion overcame them and left. The Princess Diva was not deterred by this and proceeded to perform in a beautiful gold Lemay gown with a towel dropped around her neck. After the show she proceeded to have a meet and greet with a few of the very elite high rollers of the Casino resort after about 40 minutes of taking photographs with many very guesses, she decided it was enough and didn't want to do anymore. Unfortunately, there were three young gentleman who were all under the age of 10 years old, who were devout fans and wanted to take their picture with her, but she refused. Unfortunately for her those three gentlemen were the sons of the resorts owner which put me in a precarious position to explain who they were and who is paying her paycheck. She took the photograph and then stormed away in a huff.

She was never invited back to the casino resort, and I avoided booking her for other resorts I worked with based on these interactions. The Princess Diva was traveling at the time with her family and her close friends. Her husband was a popular Rap star who was well known but living off the popularity of his wife. Her friends were mortified by her actions and made it clear that if they should have the opportunity to work with us, they would not act in a detrimental manor. They were booked in the future, and they were lovely entertainers to work with.

The Queen Diva

There once was a girl's trio that burst onto the scene and revolutionized music in the pop, R&B and disco genres. They consisted of contrasting voices that together made music history and are quoted and mimicked fifty years later. While they were strong together, they also had brilliant solo careers. The Queen Diva was well known for a powerful voice, a loving nature, and a truly mean streak.

The Queen Diva was well known to perform for hours on end if she felt the audience was responding well to her, and she was also well known to cut her show short after a half hour, if she did not feel the connection with her audience. On one evening, The Queen Diva was invited to give a free concert in Central Park in New York City. It was a beautiful summer night with well over a half of million fans screaming her name and singing along. The concert went well for about an hour until a pop-up thunderstorm appeared and the fans evacuated. The Queen Diva decided that she would continue to sing with all the electronic equipment surrounding her. After about five minutes, many concert goers had ran for shelter and lightning was now occurring in the distance. The entertainment equipment suppliers made the decision to stop all power to the venue which infuriated the Queen Diva. The next day she lambasted the city, the Central Park management, the mayor and even the fans. This was the beginning of her fall from grace that caused a near a ten-year sabbatical to Europe.

The Queen Diva was truly a magnificent singer and at the same time could be a truly horrible person, ridiculing staff members, forcing security into horrible tasks and truly forcing people when she was seen to run the other way. She was at one time the top performer and beloved by many different casino organizations, but her harshness and true nature to the staff and audience nearly cost her career to end and caused a sabbatical of well over ten years. While her entertainment was stunning to observe her true nature was nothing that anyone wanted to behold. When her trio broke up another member the Duchess Diva was also hatched with the true belief that she was as good as, if not better than, the Queen Diva, but we will examine her in a subsequent story.

When The Queen Diva returned to the stages after her sabbatical in Europe, there was a drastic change in nature and performing style. When appearing she gave a solid show with little alteration between the song list set. He reactions to her audience and her venue management were always pleasant and even gregarious at times. The changes in her attitude allowed for several residencies throughout the world and allowed her to continue to perform. We all learn with age, but The Queen Diva genuinely changed her nature and was educated by the lack of work she was offered while she was in Europe.

The Queen Of Entertainment

Growing up in the 1960s and 1970s, my musical taste ranged from the big band era (parents records) of the 1940s and 1950s to early days of rock 'n' roll to R&B and soul and then eventually to disco. As my musical tastes were eclectic (basically listened to whatever music I could get my ears on), I enjoyed much of the sounds of my neighborhood. As I lived in a true community, my friends ranged from listeners of old school opera, jive, jazz, rock, British Invasion, calypso, Latin, and my favorite R&B. Many of my friends and I would borrow albums from the family vaults to experience the varying sounds of the city (we occasionally swapped records and albums like baseball cards). That is where I first heard the beautiful voice of the Queen of Entertainment. My parents encouraged my experiencing different cultures as they had lived in the same neighborhood most of their lives and had experienced the culture changes and nuances of the community, I was now a part of. Music was a bonding force for me and my school classmates. We experienced each other's culture through the sounds of music and the smells and tastes of the foods that were offered. Spending times with other families always gave me a greater understanding of the neighborhood, and the food tasted better with the music offered.

The Queen of Entertainment was always my favorite performer, and I regret that I have only seen her three times. She was always a woman of power, of love and a true enriching SOUL. She was well known in many communities but rarely used her entertainment venues to do more than entertain and overwhelm her audiences, her gospel melodious toned voice was always true entertainment whether you were in the front row or in the back of the theater. The Queen of Entertainment rarely performed more than a few shows in any certain venue during a given week, but she always gave her heart, her soul, and her complete body to the enrichment and development of her devout fans.

One evening, in a very warm theater, The Queen of Entertainment was about halfway through her show, and she came very overheated. After one of her power ballads, she excused herself and went and stayed for fifteen minutes in her dressing room. The Queen of Entertainment sat in a bathtub, full of ice, in her gown, to cool down and not to hurt any of her audience's feelings. She then quickly changed and returned to the stage to finish off her show. Few, if any in the audience thought it was anything more than an intermission, but I was back of the house, and we were extremely concerned and apprehensive that she may have been ill or have injured herself. The Queen of Entertainment returned to the stage and belted out song after song with steam rising from her chilled skin. This was a far above and beyond what most entertainers were willing to do for their fans, but the Queen of Entertainment thought nothing out of the ordinary had occurred and she loved what she did and continued that dedication until her last soulful breath.

The Rhythm & Blues Kings Together

From The 1960s until the mid-1990s two Rhythm & Blues groups ruled the airwaves of pop and easy listening music. They were always performing their synchronized dancing, along with chart topping ballads to multitudes of fans throughout the world. These two groups were always in competition, but behind the scenes were quite friendly. As the competition was always enthusiastic, they always seemed to be trying to out-do each other. Their melodious is tones were rarely ever experienced in the same venue, as they always were discussed as if one group were the extension of another; however, they were always on different labels and always highly competitive against one another.

Over the years, much of both groups have perished, but younger members (many of whom are family members.) have joined to keep the sounds alive and the synchronicity vibrant. Over the years I have worked in many venues where I have engaged one of these groups to perform and have never been disappointed, whether it was the original artists or their replacements. These group's careers spanned many differing growth spurts in music, and the friendships that they had made brought many musical artists to their show and them to others shows. I have often been called to the rear of the showroom to escort a group member backstage to visit with these R&B Kings. The reverence that has been given to the original band members and their replacements is awe inspiring and a true testament to how music spans not only generations but musical categories.

One New Year's Eve these two groups were performing at different casino venues in the same town and a talk show host who had become a casino owner decided to have a television show broadcast from his hotel on an international stage. The talk show host had the idea to have the two groups of Rhythm and Blues Kings, all perform together, one night only. These were the original artists, from both groups, in full tuxedos, without a rehearsal. This was truly an event, not only were they on stage singing their songs, but they were also singing each other songs and dancing in synchronicity, that was unbelievable. These performers always took up the stage by themselves but together formed a line of musical genius never be duplicated. They sang for a half hour and the audience just begged for more.

Truly one of the great nights for Rhythm & Blues Kings and for the Talk Shows Host careers. This was witnessed by several thousand concert goers, and millions of people who tuned in or taped the broadcast. As this was prior to the social media boom, many of the fandom have heard of this performance but have never experienced the broadcast.

The Sad Comedian

—————

One of the great joys of working within a casino show room, is watching comedians perform to a crowd and bring them to their knees in laughter. Many comedians utilize small venues to try new material and to hone their craft. Once these comedians reach a large venue, they normally have a polished set of jokes that will entertain an audience for nearly two hours. Comedians are generally easy going and have throngs of support from friends and family that surround them. Most comedians talk of their lives, their upbringing and especially the family and friends closest to them. Comics who are from certain juris-dictions will talk of their upbringing and relate to their audience on varying levels to conjure laughter and future bookings within the given area and the venue they are presently appearing.

One comedian that I genuinely enjoyed working with, had a country music background and traveled on occasion with musical accompaniment of future Nashville artists. The support he gave to future artists was imperative to his growth as he was once a member of their fraternity that failed at musical accomplishments, but the comedic portion of his concert catapulted him to stardom. As a comedian, he realized that the audience respected him for who he was and what he said and occasionally sang to them. The future artists that accompanied him became a large part of the ensemble within the show. Music, comedy and a ruckus event were the hallmarks of the comedian's show.

The Sad Comedian was very well-suited for Midwestern audiences because they loved his down-home comedy. The Sad Comedian was always joyous and fun to be around and usually the toast of the town whenever he came to certain jurisdictions to play. Unfortunately, in his private life, some personal difficulties within his marriage and with his children had arisen. After not seeing him for about two years his management representation reached out to me and relayed that he would resume his touring schedule. When negotiating his contract, it was revealed that he would be traveling alone, no other artists, no family, no friends which was highly unusual. The Sad Comedian returned to the stage a broken jester that could not relate to his audience, his friends and the organizations he was working for. It was unfortunate because he was a very lively comedian who enjoyed doing what he did but lost a career because he could not control his anger nor change his style and unfortunately, he was no longer funny to audiences and too dark for venue managements. Eventually The Sad Comedian returned to the stage with newer material, but time can only tell if this resurgence will return his career to prominence or merely allow for him to fade away as so many others have.

The Showman

Over the course of the past century, Las Vegas has been the mecca of headliner and revue entertainment. The vaudevillian performers of the 1920's and 1930's gave way to the Big Band Era and the 1940's and 1950's. In the 1960's, the headliners continued but a group of house-revue acts also began to proliferate as casino resorts wanted to attract the abundance of visitors that were now beginning to frequent from around the world, due to cheaper and more available air transportation. As these revues bean to abound, magic, showgirls, illusions, and comedians could be found as the centerpiece of mid-week entertainment. Headliners still dominated the weekend entertainment; however, they became less and less frequent during the midweek. As casinos also moved eastward to Atlantic City in the 1970's and 1980's, these entertainment policies continued. Once the riverboat casinos and the tribal casinos abounded, entertainment became an afterthought except for special occasions. This became true in many destinations outside of the Nevada and New Jersey marketplaces, as they still were the capitals for headliners (and still are, even after the Covid pandemic).

During the fifty plus years, The Showman has performed in many different venues, but he is most well-known for his Las Vegas residencies and his truly eye-opening entertainment. He has been known to travel throughout the country and when he brings his show to different venues throughout the world he is always mobbed and beloved. The kindness he has shown to not only his fellow performers who he has helped along the way, but also his fans and the establishments in which he works can only be ruled remarkable. He believes that entertainment is the greatest form of gratitude that he can offer to any of his adoring fans, as while he has progressed to the point where he merely moderates the entertainment being performed, he still gives a solid performance, along with never ending joy to all that observe his concert. While he no longer keeps the hectic schedule that he used to, The Showman still performs well over half the year in venues throughout the world and again especially Las Vegas.

The Showman has continued to mentor and coach young performers on stage to grow and continue to groom prosperous performers through his entertainment. In a recent show, he performed for two hours along side of three budding performers. These musical artists have subsequently gone on to growing careers and are climbing the musical charts of their respective genres, all through the helping hand of The Showman. The female performers he introduced have skyrocketed on the country and pop-rock charts while the young gentleman has found success reveling in the "American Songbook." The three talents are vastly differing, but their success in uniquely attributed to the Showman.

The adage that those who cannot do—teach, does not hold true of The Showman, rather those who have experienced success—

should reach back and help others forward. The Showman—The Mentor—The driving force for new entertainment.

The Crooner's Favorite Voice

During the era of the great American Songbook, many of the entertainers of the day performed each other songs. The Crooner as we had mentioned prior was the king of this era, but rarely would he perform this noble man's songs because he genuinely enjoyed the performers voice and would not replace his inflections. Over the years, the Crooner 's Favorite Voice evolved into an icon himself, being known to perform and outshine many of his contemporaries. Having shared the stage with many of the titans of entertainment, he always held the distinction of being the most recognized voice in the ensemble. He has done duets with many of the past and present performers and has outsold many musical icons throughout time.

On a spectacular night, the favorite voice moved to the front of the stage of an exceptionally large opera house and proceeded to sing a cappella to the entire audience without using a microphone. The guests of the upper balcony could only echo the sentiments of everyone in the opera house to the melodious nature of his voice and sealed his greatness in musical history. While this was the first time, I had witnessed this achievement, this was not the first time he had performed this accomplishment as he loved the "opera house effect" and had one of only a few voices who could perform and have perfect pitch without the use of any audio equipment. As the crowd roared with applause, he gently picked up his microphone and continued the show as if nothing out of the ordinary had occurred.

During meet-and-greets with select fans (in my case high roller guests) he had a strict rule of only taking photographs with a select number. When that number had been reached, he politely thanks the group and makes his exit. Some guests have been offended by this, but he always apologizes in advance, giving the number of people that he will take photographs with and promptly leaving when the number was reached. Therefore, it was always the responsibility of the resort organization to not overload the special event. One of the funniest stories was during a meet-and-greets, he literally has his manager stay in there to count the number of people that he is going to take pictures with and when that number is reached, he sang a song as he departed ("Goodnight Irene"). I have attended meet-and-greets with this gentleman over ten times, and I do not have a photo with him.

Over the course of the years, he has performed duets with many up-and-coming entertainers and famous performers of his time and is truly remembered as one of the supreme entertainers to have graced to stage. His voice is as strong and recognizable at the end of his career as it was when he began over sixty years ago. He was a gentleman to work with, a superb artist to relish and a hysterical prankster to witness, with his antics.

About the Author

 Anthony "Bert" Bertino is an innovative team marketing professional who blazed an innovative path in Marketing, Special Events, Advertising, Digital Marketing, Digital Media, Marketing Strategy, Social Media Marketing, Public Relations, Brand Management, Communications, Integrated Marketing, Market Analysis, Online Advertising, Online Marketing and Player Development within the gaming industry for over forty years.

Bert has a strong tendency to work toward making things happen rather than waiting for things to happen. He set high goals, then works hard with people to achieve those goals. Bert is an entrepreneur who consulted with gaming organizations, whether it be land-based, riverboat or tribal, to enhance market share, create a positive, nurturing atmosphere, and mentoring of staff and organization.

Bert believes that all employees are ambassadors and hosts for their organization. Bert believes that all customers are important to the facility, be it from group sales, conventioneers, existing customers and new players. Bert demands high performance of himself and others.

Bert was always a fan of short stories and providing life lessons from short story examples. Studs Terkel book "Working" 1974, was a driving force in writing this book as it explained the unvarnished truth about people, no judgement, no names just stories for examples.

Bert has been an adjunct professor with colleges and universities throughout the United States and teaches from the perspective of this is what I observed and how I processed the situation. This has all been accomplished through first hand accounts relayed through short stories.